The ABCs of Investment Banking

Written by Amit Saraf, Varun Bhartia, and Raamin Mostaghimi

Illustrated by Kyle Navaluna

For Sohan, Shaily, Roya, Sohan, Riya, and Ravi

A special thank you to all those that contributed, reviewed drafts, and tested on their children:
Kristen Young

Copyright © 2018 Very Young Professionals Publishing
www.veryyoungprofessionals.com

All rights reserved
ISBN-13:
978-1-7325217-5-9

A is for **all-nighter**

When you're about to close an important deal, you might have to pull an **all-nighter**, and work so hard you don't get to sleep! Your VP might join you, but never your MD.

B is for bulge bracket or boutique

Bulge bracket banks work with many different financial products, and *boutique banks* work with fewer, more specific financial products. No matter where you work, you're going to be updating slides and spreadsheets.

C is for circular reference

*A **circular reference** is a never-ending loop in your spreadsheet that will haunt you even in your dreams.*

D is for **dealmaker**

You can't really be a **dealmaker** if you spend all your time updating spreadsheets – but you sure can call yourself one!

E is for EBITDA

A complicated-sounding term that just means how much money your company makes. By saying "EBITDA", you'll make your clients think you're super fancy.

F is for Friday at 5pm

*Sometimes it seems like **Friday at 5pm** is the only time your MD and VP are allowed to give you additional work - even if they knew about it three days ago.*

G is for GAAP

*GAAP is a way of measuring company earnings - it stands for **Generally Accepted Accounting Principles**. When GAAP is too low, a skillful investment banker will focus investors on non-GAAP earnings.*

H is for hedge

*An investment banker might **hedge** a deal for a client - which helps them make money no matter whether the deal turns out good or bad. This has the added benefit of letting the banker charge even more fees!*

I is for Initial Public Offering (IPO)

*In an **Initial Public Offering**, or **IPO**, a private company will look to raise money from the public markets with the help of an investment banker. They may also rent a fancy private plane for everyone to fly in.*

J is for **junk bonds**

Junk bonds are issued by companies that have fallen on hard times. They are often sold under the better sounding name of "High-Yield Bonds"

K is for 10-K

A **10-K** is a document every investment banker pretends to have read that contains lots of useful information about their public clients.

L is for league table

League tables are a set of rankings which help CEOs and CFOs choose the best investment banker for the job, by letting them show off how many deals they've done.

M is for **merger**

When two companies really like each other, they may look to conduct a **merger** and become one big, strong company. Investment bankers are really helpful to make this happen.

N is for net present value

*One way investment bankers guess the value of a company is by doing a **net present value** calculation - you have to be really good at math to get these right!*

O is for **on a deal**

It is often more exciting for an investment banker to be **on a deal** versus pitching ideas to a client, however, both are really important functions.

P is for private equity

*A **private equity** firm is a place that is often staffed with many former investment bankers, so it is really important for investment bankers to be really nice to these folks.*

Q is for **quitting time**

Quitting time is a mythical concept that never actually seems to take place in the world of investment banking.

R is for regulations

There are many rules, also known as **regulations**, that investment bankers must follow. If they break any one of them, both the bankers and their clients could be in a lot of trouble.

S is for Sales and Traders

*There are many types of investment bankers - corporate financiers do super big deals, while **sales and traders** do lots of smaller deals every day. All investment bankers, though, try to get a big year-end bonus.*

T is for **take-out dinner**

*Associate Alligator often works late into the evening. When this happens, she can order **take-out dinner** using her expense account and bring leftovers for her friends and family.*

U is for upgrade

A flight **upgrade** for a work trip can be fun, but sometimes it only happens for Managing Directors.

V is for valuation

*Whether it is based on a detailed financial analysis by Associate Alligator, or just a gut feel by Managing Director Monkey, an investment banker always has a view on **valuation**.*

W is for Wall Street

While investment bankers are located and work all over the world, they all proudly get to say they work on "**Wall Street**".

X is for **eXtra attention to detail**

*Every investment banker must have **eXtra attention to detail**, as a single miscalculation can cause a client to lose of millions of dollars. Even worse, it can result in a lower year-end bonus.*

Y is for year-end bonus

*The **year-end bonus** is the single figure bankers point to when they explain to friends and family why they were working on Thanksgiving (and other holidays).*

Z is for zzzzz's

*If no one else is in the office after midnight, Analyst Armadillo may catch some **zzzzz's** for a few hours, and still tell his deal team he pulled an all-nighter.*

Thank you for reading!